Working Together Against

THE DESTRUCTION OF THE ENVIRONMENT

Many cities, like Los Angeles, have taken important steps toward solving
their pollution problems.

❖THE LIBRARY OF SOCIAL ACTIVISM❖

Working Together Against

THE DESTRUCTION OF THE ENVIRONMENT

By Robert Gartner

THE ROSEN PUBLISHING GROUP, INC.
NEW YORK

For my daughter Amy, and her cousins Chris, Nickie, Taryn, Erin, Hunter, Brandon, Cari, Molly, and Peter, who are working together to help save the environment.

Published in 1994 by The Rosen Publishing Group, Inc.
29 East 21st Street, New York, NY 10010

First Edition

Library of Congress Cataloging-in-Publication Data

Gartner, Robert.
    Working together against the destruction of the environment / by Robert Gartner.
        p.   cm. — (The Library of social activism)
    Includes bibliographical references and index.
    ISBN 0-8239-1774-6
    1. Environmentalism—Juvenile literature.   2. Environmental degradation—Juvenile literature.   3. Man—Influence on nature—Juvenile literature.   [1. Environmental protection.
2. Environmental degradation.   3. Pollution.]   I. Title.
II. Title: Destruction of the environment.   III. Series.
GE195.5.G37   1994
363.7—dc20   94-2278
                                                                              CIP
                                                                              AC

Manufactured in the United States of America

Contents

INTRODUCTION

THE EARTH IS IN SERIOUS TROUBLE. THE countries of the world have misused their natural resources and polluted the earth and the air around it. The ability of the earth to support life has been diminished. The earth and the air make up our environment—that is, all the external conditions and influences surrounding us and influencing our life.

The news is full of scary stories about the environment. In the 1970s in the community of Love Canal, New York, people were getting sick. The townspeople discovered that a business had buried toxic waste in the ground. The deadly chemicals were seeping into the town's water supply.

In some parts of the United States, the weather reports recommend that people who have breathing problems stay inside because the air pollution is worse than usual.

Is it too late to save the earth? What can you,

one person, do? It's not too late, but the earth needs our help now. We can make a big difference. This book will show you some ways we can help save the earth.

The condition of the environment affects every living person, plant, and animal on earth. We must all work together to make the earth a safe and healthy place to live.

The favorable conditions that existed before we humans started polluting, can be reestablished to a great degree, and your generation has the power to help heal the earth.

❖ QUESTIONS TO ASK YOURSELF ❖

The condition of the environment affects every living being on earth. It is important that we, as humans, learn how to protect and restore it. Let's explore how it concerns you. 1) In what ways do you enjoy the environment? Do you like to hike, fish, swim, or camp? Do you like to drink clean water or breathe fresh air? 2) How are the ways you like to enjoy the environment affected by pollution?

In some cities, pollution has reached such high levels that residents must wear protective masks.

chapter

1

EVERYTHING IS CONNECTED

"ALL THINGS ARE CONNECTED. EVERYTHING IS a circle" said Chief Seattle of the Suquamish Indian Tribe in 1854. Today, Native Americans often quote Chief Seattle when referring to the environment and the problems the earth is facing. The word environment comes from the Latin word, viron, which means circle. All living creatures and plants; the air, land, and water, are connected and when something happens to one of them, it can start a chain reaction that affects all the others.

As an example of a chain reaction, consider the trees, and our relationship to them. Through a process called photosynthesis, each tree leaf converts sunlight into energy, and uses the gas, carbon dioxide (CO_2), in the process. The leaf soaks up carbon dioxide given off by animals. Carbon dioxide is also present in the exhaust from cars and trucks, but we don't need this source. The leaf produces starches and sugars

and releases oxygen into the air. We, in turn, take in the oxygen and the cycle continues.

Trees also anchor the soil. Decaying leaves decompose on the ground, forming humus, an organic material which helps make the soil fertile.

When trees are cut down, the soil is no longer held down and either blows away or is easily washed away by rainstorms. Rain carries the particles of soil into rivers and lakes. Dirt settling on the bottoms of rivers or lakes is called silt. Silt in rivers covers the spawning beds of fish and suffocates the fish eggs and the aquatic insects.

If the fish eggs can't hatch, the fish population disappears. Birds and animals that feed on fish move elsewhere, looking for more abundant food. The chain reactions in the river continue but we'll stop here.

Back on land, the result of having fewer trees is that less CO_2 is processed to release oxygen, and the CO_2 remains in the atmosphere. The increase in CO_2 is one of the causes of global warming. Global warming starts another series of chain reactions.

You can start understanding these connections when you look at the individual environmental problems. You can study one problem and see how it is related to other problems, and come up with some simple solutions. Going

back to our example of the trees—when they are cut down, CO_2 accumulates, less oxygen is released, and air pollution spreads. Soil is washed away, plant and animal species are lost and the destruction continues. The solution is to plant more trees and save the ones we already have. By planting trees and managing them, we are working to reduce a number of environmental problems.

Chief Seattle was a wise man. His people lived near Puget Sound, in harmony with the earth. Chief Seattle also said, "To harm the earth is to heap contempt upon its creator. Whatever happens to the earth happens to the children of the earth."

Pollution of the air, the soil, the fresh waters and the oceans is a serious threat to the health and survival of humans and all other living species. Our bodies are made up of the chemical and mineral elements and gases of the earth. By breathing, eating, and drinking, we take into our bodies the air, food, and water of the earth. As the earth becomes more polluted, so do we. The soil itself is dying. The organisms in the soil are being killed off.

That isn't a pleasant thought, and pollution isn't a pleasant sight. Have you ever sat on a riverbank and then left because the smell of the river and the sight of floating garbage drove you away? Have you ever tried to fish in a fishless

Water pollution includes anything from invisible chemicals to actual garbage.

lake? Some beautiful lakes are fishless because acid rain has killed every living organism in them. Visitors to the Grand Canyon often can't see from one rim to the other because of the dirty air.

Because everything is connected, anything that you do to help the environment is a vital step toward saving the earth. Don't get discouraged because the problems are difficult to understand and seem too big to tackle. One person's actions can make a tremendous difference.

**Everything is
Connected**

By learning more about the environment you
can come to understand many of the complex
connections. Through hands-on projects in your
community, you will see that your actions do
make a difference. Your goal as you go about
your everyday life should be to leave the earth in
better condition than you found it.

❖ QUESTIONS TO ASK YOURSELF ❖

The environment is one big circle of chain
reactions. Each being has an effect on other
beings. 1) If every living thing is connected,
how do you as a human being fit into the circle?
2) Are there pollution problems where you live?
What are they?

chapter

2

THE PROBLEMS

MANY OF THE PROBLEMS WE READ OR HEAR about are confusing. What is global warming and how does it affect us? What is the ozone layer and who cares if it has a hole in it?

You don't have to be a scientist to start working to correct the environmental problems. Here is a brief description of some of the problems the earth is facing:

Too Much Garbage—each person in the United States throws away more than 1,200 pounds of garbage per year. Most of the garbage ends up in landfills or dumps. Landfill sites are filling up and many cities are running out of places to store garbage.

Air Pollution—the main cause of air pollution is the exhaust from cars and the burning of coal for the production of electricity. Even though cars pollute less than they used to, there are more cars than ever, and people are driving more miles. When the air is dirty, it is uncom-

Each person in the United States produces 1,200 pounds
of garbage each year.

fortable to breathe and dangerous to our health.
Over 110 million people in the U.S. live in areas
where it is often unhealthy to breathe the air.

Acid Rain—When fossil fuels such as gaso-
line and coal are burned, sulfur dioxides and
nitrogen oxides are released into the air. They
combine with chemicals in the air and in the
presence of moisture, form sulfuric acid. This
acid falls back to Earth. Acid rain or snow
destroys plant and animal life in streams and
lakes, kills trees, and even corrodes buildings

and statues. It irritates our eyes and skin and internal organs. Due to acid rain more than 2,200 of Sweden's freshwater lakes are lifeless.

Decreased Ozone Layer—ozone is a gas that forms a protective shield around the earth. The ozone layer prevents the sun from burning the earth. Without the ozone layer much more ultraviolet light would reach us. The increased ultraviolet radiation would cause skin cancer, damage eyes, destroy farm crops, and reduce fish populations. The ozone layer is being destroyed by chemicals called chlorofluorocarbons (KLOR-o-floor-o-CAR-bons) or CFCs for short. CFCs are used in the manufacture of many products, including styrofoam packaging materials (the kind McDonalds used to use for their hamburgers). When CFCs are released into the atmosphere, they mix with sunlight and release chlorine atoms. The chlorine atoms destroy ozone.

The Greenhouse Effect—the air around the earth is called the atmosphere. When the sun shines, some of the heat reaches the ground and some of it rises back into outer space. Carbon dioxide, nitrogen oxide, CFCs, and methane are gases in the atmosphere which trap the sun's heat. This is causing global warming. Some of the effects of excessive global warming would be the melting of ice around the North and South Poles and the consequent rising of sea levels.

Many cities would flood. Some areas would be too hot to live in.

Water Pollution—our water comes from lakes, rivers, and underground water. Many of these waters have become polluted by fertilizers, pesticides, and the careless disposal of hazardous materials. Worldwide, almost 1.2 billion people are without safe drinking water.

Vanishing Wildlife—the pollution of the earth is driving many animals from their homes. Some of them cannot adapt to new habitats, and die. Scientists estimate that one hundred species a year are becoming extinct.

Rain forests—rain forests occupy less than ten percent of the earth's surface, but contain about fifty percent of the trees on earth and forty percent of the world's biodiversity. Rain forest trees and plants are the source of many medicines. Rain forests absorb CO_2 and release oxygen. It is important to save them if we are to stop global warming. These forests are being destroyed at the rate of one football field per second, or forty-two million acres a year. The Amazon Basin is the largest remaining tropical rain forest.

Deforestation—in the U.S., only one tree is planted for every four that die or are cut down. Trees anchor the soil and prevent soil erosion and just as importantly, they soak up CO_2 and release oxygen.

The burning of rain forests affects the entire ecosystem.

Overpopulation—today's world population numbers 5.4 billion. By the year 2050, the population could be 12.5 billion.

These are just a small sampling of the problems we face. There are several books available that provide a fuller explanation of these problems and suggest actions you can take to help solve them. Two of these are *The Kids' Earth Handbook* by Sandra Markle and *Save The Earth: An Action Handbook For Kids* by Betty Miles. Another book that everyone should read is

50 Simple Things You Can Do To Save The Earth, published by Earth Works Press.

Every one of us is a victim of the damaged environment. We breathe foul air. We eat foods containing chemical preservatives and large traces of dozens of pesticides. Our meat is contaminated with steroids and antibiotics. We swim and fish in dirty waters. Each of these environmental problems is reducing the quality of our lives.

The odd thing is that we buy products that are supposed to make life easier and improve the quality of our lives. But by using these products, we are damaging the environment and reducing the quality of our lives. Do we really need things like electric can openers and electric pencil sharpeners? Yes, they are fast but they also use electricity. One of the main causes of air pollution is the generating of electricity.

There are thousands of products that are convenient but unnecessary, and the packaging alone is tremendously wasteful. Have you bought a compact disc lately? Much of the packaging on CDs is needless and just adds to the mountains of garbage.

The cost of cleaning up pollution is staggering. In the United States, the Department of Commerce estimates that the overall cost of dealing with air pollution exceeds thirty-two billion dollars a year. The Swedish Government

spends more than fifty million dollars a year trying to reverse the effects of acid rain. They are adding huge amounts of lime to the lakes to neutralize the acids.

Who ends up paying for this? We do. Companies charge more for their products in order to pay for pollution control. The government uses money from our taxes to pay for environmental cleanups. If the environment were clean, the government could use the money for other programs, like providing decent permanent housing for the homeless.

But the environment isn't clean and these problems can't be solved overnight. The cleanup will take a long time but it can be done. We have used and abused the earth's resources. The earth does not belong to us. We belong to the earth.

❖ **QUESTIONS TO ASK YOURSELF** ❖

Sometimes it seems like everything we do causes pollution. Let's take a look this. 1) What have you thrown away as garbage today? 2) How might you have recycled some of that garbage?

chapter

3

HOW YOU CAN HELP

WITH OVER FIVE BILLION PEOPLE IN THE
world, it is hard to believe that your individual
contribution in working to save the earth can
make a difference. "What can one person do?"
you may ask. But you are not alone in this
effort. There is a growing sense of urgency about
environmental problems. Most people around
the globe stand firmly behind efforts to clean the
environment.

More and more Americans are becoming
concerned enough to take action in order to
save the earth. A New York Times poll in 1989
reported that eighty percent of those polled
agreed that "protecting the environment is so
important that environmental standards cannot
be set too high and that environmental improvements should be made regardless of the cost."

Not only are more people concerned but
they are turning their concern into action to
improve the earth. To help you get started,

Earth Day is an annual event designed to mobilize people around environmental issues.

environmental workers have a saying that can guide your efforts: Think Globally, Act Locally.

Thinking globally, means you are aware of all the nations of the earth and their major problems, and how these problems affect everyone on earth. Remember Chief Seattle's words, "All things are connected." Acting locally means doing whatever you can, right where you are, to save the earth. Learn about the local aspects of global issues.

Endangered species are a global issue. Are

there endangered species living in or near your area? What can you do to help them? Can you improve their habitat in any way? Air and water pollution are global issues. How does your community dispose of its waste? Are there local industries or farms which pollute the air, water, or land? Think about what you can do to get the polluters to stop. By picking up litter, conserving water, recycling paper and glass, building shelters for wildlife, or planting trees, you are taking positive action in your local area. You are doing something, no matter how small, to help the environment.

Think Globally, Act Locally should be the key to your community activities. Acting locally will increase peoples' awareness of global problems. As more people get involved in your earth-saving projects, they will be inspired to recruit friends and this will add to the army of Earth's defenders.

The book, *50 Simple Things Kids Can Do To Save the Earth* is full of information and projects that anyone can do. Most of the projects are things you can do around your house or in your community. You will see the immediate effect of your actions.

As you get involved in different projects, continue to study more about the earth and its problems. Learn how things work together, how everything and everybody are connected. Get

The northern spotted owl is one of many species threatened by environmental changes.

books from the library, watch nature shows on television and join an environmental group.

There are hundreds of environmental groups in the United States. Most groups have monthly meetings that are open to everyone and these groups are usually involved with projects that you can help with. They are always glad to have more help. Some organizations, like the National Wildlife Federation, have special programs and magazines for kids and young adults.

It's also important to write letters to your

mayor and city council members, to your county
and state officials, and to your senators and representatives in Congress. The library will have
their addresses. Tell these people about your
concerns and that you want laws to support
recycling, to protect forests, to stop pollution
and the dumping of toxic waste. Be as specific
as possible when you are writing about a local
problem. For example, instead of saying that
you are worried about air pollution, say that
you're worried about the air pollution from the
factories in your city. Name those factories.
Write to a company that is polluting in your
area and tell them about the effects of their pollution and ask them to stop. Call up and ask
who the president of that company is, and write
to that person.

One letter can do a lot. Most people don't
take the time to sit down and write to elected
officials or to businesses. Get your friends and
family to write also. When elected officials re-
ceive a lot of letters on one subject, it moves
them to give consideration to that subject. The
mail acts as a reminder to them that they were
elected to serve the people, and that the people
are watching.

Your letter should be short and direct, one
page if possible. State your concerns and your
position politely and why the issue is important.
Always ask for a response so you know where

Paper mills are a major source of air pollution.

your elected official stands on an issue. If you write to a business about a problem, ask them for a response explaining what they plan to do about the problem.

Here is a sample letter to a United States Senator asking for support in the renewal of the Clean Water Act.

LASHAWN DAVIS
243 MAIN STREET MY TOWN, NE 0220502
PHONE NUMBER HERE

Date here
The Honorable _____
U.S. Senate
Washington, D.C. 20510

Dear Senator _____ :

I am asking you to vote for the renewal of the Clean Water Act. Because of the Clean Water Act, many of the rivers in the United States are now safe for drinking, swimming and fishing.

This law is helping to clean up the _____ River which flows through our town. Please let me know your position on renewing the Clean Water Act.
Sincerely,

LaShawn Davis

Depending on the issue, the letter can be longer and you can add some personal experiences, but try to keep it to one page.

You should also write to your Congress person. Address the letter to:

The Honorable _____
U.S. House of Representatives
Washington, D.C. 20515

No matter how hard you work on a project, it is important to remember that it may take years before you see any positive changes. This is especially true with projects involving the land, such as reforesting an area. You will not see immediate results and it will be years before changes are evident. Don't get discouraged. Solving problems like climate change, ozone depletion, and acid rain, requires our long term commitment.

Become a green consumer. Purchase products that are made from recycled materials. Read all labels and tags and information on packages very carefully. The language is often deceiving. Look up ingredients in library reference books. The librarian will tell you which books to look in.

Avoid companies that pollute the environment and products that are harmful to the environment. Write a letter to the president of the company and let him or her know why you won't buy their product. If enough people wrote letters, business would become environmentally responsible. Because of kids' efforts, McDonalds stopped using styrofoam packaging.

Throughout your life, continue to learn as much as possible about the environment and how to save the earth. The more you learn, the easier it will be to think up your own projects. Remember the key: Think Globally, Act Locally.

❖ QUESTIONS TO ASK YOURSELF ❖

To begin thinking globally and acting locally, think about the answers to these questions.
1) On a scale of one to ten, where would you rank the importance of the environment to you?
2) What is the biggest environmental problem in your community? 3) Who are your local senators and representatives? Where do they stand on issues involving the environment?

chapter

4

THE ENVIRONMENTAL MOVEMENT

THE ENVIRONMENTAL MOVEMENT BEGAN IN THE 1960s when people became alarmed and began to work actively to improve the earth. The movement started in the United States and spread across the world in response to the misuse and overuse of natural resources. "Growth at all costs—anything goes" was the prevailing philosophy. The pollution of the air and water, the deforesting of the land, the tons of garbage, and the poisoning of the land by pesticides and chemical fertilizers caused many Americans to stop and think. Most people now realize that our natural resources are not limitless.

John Muir was a naturalist who, over one hundred years ago, explored California's Sierra Nevada mountains and the area that later became Yosemite National Park. He is considered by many to be our first environmental leader. He was the first person to propose that certain natural areas be set aside as wilderness areas. A wilderness area does not have any roads, houses, or any other development and is permanently maintained in its natural state.

Many people are willing to demonstrate their concern for the environment.

John Muir was a founder of the Sierra Club, one of the world's leading environmental organizations. Other thinkers and activists who helped build the foundation for today's environmentalism include Henry David Thoreau, Ralph Waldo Emerson, Frederick Law Olmstead, President Theodore Roosevelt, Gifford Pinchot, Rachel Carson, and Francis Moore Lappe. They were among the first to teach us that if we are to save ourselves, we must first stop destroying the earth.

In 1916, the National Park Service was created to manage the national parks in America. The first two were Yellowstone and Yosemite. The National Park Service has grown to manage 360 parks. These include historic battlefields, birthplaces and homes of presidents, monuments, wild and scenic rivers, and seashores.

The continuing destruction of the earth's natural resources and the environmental activism that began in the 1960s, led Wisconsin Senator Gaylord Nelson to establish the first Earth Day celebration on April 22, 1970. In ceremonies across the United States the message that day was "We have only one earth and we'd better take care of it." More than twenty million Americans took part in activities that day and learned about ways to care for the earth.

Earth Day has changed the way people think about the environment. People now consider a clean and protected environment as important to their happiness as their constitutional rights.

Biking is healthy both for you and the environment. Environment
Protection Agency Administrator Carol Browner and other
EPA employees biked to work in celebration of Earth Day.

In the years following Earth Day, 1970, environmentalism has grown into a mass movement in America and received increasing coverage in the media. It has come to be known as the Green Movement.

Americans have let their Congressional representatives know how important the environment is to them. In the 1970s Congress responded by passing a series of laws to stop the destruction of the environment. Among the laws passed were the Clean Air Act, the Clean Water Act, the Endangered Species Act, the Noise Control Act, the Safe Drinking Water Act, and the National Environmental Policy Act (NEPA).

Congress created the Environmental Protection Agency (EPA) to be the federal government's watchdog and chief weapon against all forms of pollution. The EPA's job is to keep businesses, cities, and states from polluting the environment. The EPA enforces the environmental laws. It also explains the laws and provides information and assistance to help people follow the laws. The EPA identifies sources of danger and informs and educates us on how to protect ourselves and the environment.

The environmental movement has spread across the globe. The second Earth Day was on April 22, 1990. Two hundred million people in over 140 countries made their concerns about the earth known to their countries' leaders.

In response, world leaders gathered in Rio de

Janeiro in Brazil in June, 1992, for the first United Nations Conference on Environment and Development. This was also known as the Earth Summit. Probably the most important accomplishment of the Earth Summit was that world leaders recognized the environmental problems as important social and political issues.

Since the second Earth Day, many national organizations and local communities sponsor Earth Day activities annually. The National Parks and Conservation Association sponsors a nationwide March for Parks to raise money for park projects across the country. Fairfax County, Virginia, sponsors a Conservation Fair where environmental groups display information about their goals and activities. Admission to this fair is one bag of recyclable materials.

The Environmental Movement continues to grow. Environmental groups have increased membership by three hundred percent since 1980 and have become a political force. If you are doing even one thing to help the earth, you are part of this important movement.

❖ QUESTIONS TO ASK YOURSELF ❖

The environmental movement is worldwide. Let's look at some of the issues this raises. 1) Do you think nations should work together or separately on environmental issues? 2) What are some international environmental groups? What have they accomplished?

chapter

5

WHAT IS BEING DONE

THE CONDITION OF THE EARTH AND ITS environment is now front page news. Stories about the environment are often featured on national television. We should be glad that the destruction of the environment has become a big concern. Most of the time the news is bad. For example an oil tanker ruptures or toxic wastes leak into a river, or the air pollution at Grand Canyon National Park is worse than ever.

Good things are happening too but media barely publicizes the good news. What is currently being done to improve the environment?

President Clinton and Vice-President Gore are taking action to help the environment. The Vice-President has long been an environmental activist. The President has signed an international biodiversity treaty that seeks to protect plant and animal life worldwide. He has also committed the United States to help prevent further global warming by reducing emissions of greenhouse gases.

President Bill Clinton and Vice President Al Gore are making sure that the United States plays its part in protecting the environment.

The President also believes the federal government should be a model for green consumerism. He has signed an order instructing the government agencies to buy more recycled products and to replace thousands of polluting vehicles with those that run on electricity, as well as on cleaner fuels, such as natural gas and ethanol.

Environmental groups are pushing for tougher laws. They want higher environmental

standards. For example, the Clean Air Act requires that industry reduce the amount of air-polluting emissions from their smokestacks. The environmental groups want these emissions reduced even more.

The groups are also working to maintain the Endangered Species Act. Business and industry often complain that protection of endangered species halts their progress. They want the act weakened to allow for a certain amount of development even though the development may destroy the habitats of endangered species. Many people are concerned about the right to pollute, which businesses can sell to each other.

Environmental groups are the watchdogs for the earth. They are constantly monitoring legislation proposed by Congress and by the states to determine if the earth would be helped or harmed by these actions. They notify their members to support or fight the legislation by writing to their senators and representatives.

The number of new departments and agencies for protecting the environment has greatly increased at the state and local levels, since 1970. State governments are enforcing the environmental standards set by the Environmental Protection Agency. The EPA is a federal agency. In some cases, the state standards are higher than those set by the EPA.

County governments are starting recycling

programs for paper, glass, and plastic. Counties are running out of space for landfills, and in some cases, this forces them to recycle. Anti-dumping laws have been passed, and wastes like used oil, must be taken to gas stations for recycling.

Many newspapers and television stations now have a full-time environmental reporter, and feature-articles about the environment are commonplace. Magazines and videos specializing in environmental stories are now available.

Much of what is being done has happened because citizens have lobbied their elected officials for action. We all know that we need to do more. Working for the earth is a lifetime assignment.

❖ QUESTIONS TO ASK YOURSELF ❖

The United States has taken many steps toward ending the destruction of the environment. Lets think about what's been done so far. 1) What actions have President Clinton and Vice-President Gore taken? 2) What does the Clean Air Act require? 3) Can you think of areas that have not been addressed?

chapter

6

VOLUNTEER EFFORTS

GOVERNMENTS AND INDUSTRIES CAN SPEND
billions of dollars trying to clean up and restore
the environment but it won't be enough unless
one more ingredient is added. That ingredient is
you. You and your family, friends, and classmates are needed to help the earth.

In addition to your personal projects, consider volunteering to help a national or local
environmental organization. Volunteers are the
heart of these groups, which usually have only
a small paid staff. Even large groups like the
Sierra Club, the National Wildlife Federation,
and the National Audubon Society depend on
volunteers.

Most environmental groups charge a membership fee, usually under twenty-five dollars.
Some have smaller fees for students. Most of
them publish magazines or newsletters to
inform people of their activities and of important legislation under consideration. Part of

Some environmental organizations focus on preserving water resources.

your membership fee enables these groups to
work to convince legislators to vote for environmental laws. Representatives of these groups go
to Washington, and talk directly to legislators.
This is called lobbying.

There are hundreds of environmental organizations in the United States. Some of them
focus on just one issue such as the preservation
of the rain forests (Rain Forest Action Network)
or saving rivers from being dammed (American
Rivers). Others are concerned with the whole
environment and are against anything that will

41

harm it. They use many different methods to accomplish their goals. Some groups specialize in lobbying and taking court action while others sponsor research and public education programs.

If you want to join one, pick one that focuses on something that is especially interesting to you. If you like to fish and are concerned about clean lakes and rivers, Trout Unlimited (TU), the Federation of Fly Fishers (FFF), Bass Anglers Sportsman Society (BASS), and the Izaak Walton League of America are for you. They are all working to improve the condition of our country's waters. They all sponsor various projects and activities including research for fisheries and the restoration of streams.

If you want to help wildlife, the Defenders of Wildlife, the National Wildlife Federation, and the World Wildlife Fund are for you. They are working to preserve wildlife habitats and to save endangered species. Are you concerned about our national parks? If you are, join the National Parks and Conservation Association, whose goal is to preserve and expand the national park system.

There is something for everyone among the environmental groups. An excellent guide book is *The Conservation Directory* published by the National Wildlife Federation. This directory lists information about thousands of national, state, and local environmental groups. It provides names, addresses, and phone numbers and gives a short description of each group and what it does. It also lists the federal agencies that manage natural resources. The directory is updated annually. Libraries should have it, or you can purchase it from the National Wildlife Federation, 1400 16th St. NW, Washington, D.C., 20036, phone: 202 797 6800.

Most of the federal agencies and many of the environmental groups listed offer free pamphlets, brochures, or reprints of articles. The U.S. Fish and Wildlife Service has many free publications about endangered species. The Environmental Protection Agency offers free publications on a variety of subjects. For example, you can send for *Citizens Guide To Pesticides* and *Hazardous Waste Management*. Write to the groups in the directory for a list of their free publications.

Joining an environmental group is a start. Attend the group's meetings and take part in the activities. You'll meet other people with similar interests. Once you get involved in an activity or project, you'll have the satisfaction of accomplishing something for the good of the earth.

Let's look at a volunteer project. Amy and Chris are cousins. They are high school students who have adopted a stream in their town. They like to fish for trout in the stream and they also

Your own neighborhood can provide opportunities for environmental action.

enjoy walking along the bank of the stream and watching the otters play.

They have talked about the stream and how they hope it will always be safe from pollution and development. Whenever they go to the stream, they pick up any litter they find.

During Earth Week, the nearby college had held a conservation fair. Chris and Amy had stopped at the Izaak Walton League of America exhibit and learned about the Save Our Streams (SOS) Program.

They immediately signed up and adopted a stream. They received a water testing kit from the League, instructions on how to test the water, and who to notify if the quality was poor. They took turns testing the water, which had to be done twice a week.

SOS encourages individuals or groups to help maintain good water quality by adopting a stream and agreeing to watch it for a year or more. Volunteers look for problems which might lead to the decline of the stream such as erosion, trash, oil slicks, sewage leaks or abandoned storage drums. The Save Our Streams Program provides information on how to identify harmful conditions as well as how to fight them.

SOS has developed a simple, scientific way to capture and identify insects to determine a stream's health. Some insects, like mayflies and hellgrammites are extra sensitive to pollution and need high levels of oxygen.

Amy and Chris use the SOS survey method to rate the water quality. They capture aquatic insects, to record data about them. They also check and record the water temperature. If the water temperature goes above seventy degrees, the trout will have difficulty breathing and they could die.

As part of a school science project, Amy and Chris took their class to the stream and demonstrated what they were doing to protect it. They told their classmates that the stream needed more protection and more friends. The class

decided to join the effort to help the stream and discussed what they could do.

Because the stream was on county land, they went to the county planning commission and asked that it be placed under legal protection. They also received permission to do some planting in order to create more shade, thereby keeping the water temperature cool. They also wanted to increase the oxygen in the water by placing rocks and boulders in the stream. Flowing water is broken up by rocks and boulders and mixes with the air to carry oxygen into the water. Insects and fish need oxygen.

The class asked the State Fish Commission for help in designing the stream improvement projects. A fisheries biologist met with the class one Saturday and walked along the stream with them. She made some good suggestions and offered to look at their plan. The Commission also offered to help them do the work.

They developed a plan that included an estimate of the materials needed. Once the biologist approved it, the class set to work. They went to local lumber yards, gravel pits, and plant nurseries, explained what they were doing, and asked for donations of materials.

For the next two months, they spent every Saturday placing large rocks along the streambank, and planting trees. The rocks and trees stabilize the bank of the stream and prevent soil

from washing into it. The trees as they grow provide shade which will lower the water temperature. They placed gravel on the bottom of the stream to provide spawning beds for the trout. They placed boulders throughout the stream to break the flow of the current. This puts more oxygen into the water. The fish also benefit, as they can rest behind the boulders. They also built log cribs extending from the shore into the stream. This deflects the flow and breaks the fast water into riffles.

Amy and Chris called the local newspaper and told a reporter about the class project. The reporter and a photographer arrived on the day they started work and interviewed the students. The story and photographs in the paper attracted plenty of interest. Each week, more adults came to help the students.

After the basic work was completed, the class continued to pick up litter each week and monitor the water quality. Chris and Amy showed the class how to catch trout by using hooks that don't injure the trout and trout flies which imitate the insects in the stream. More importantly, they taught the class that it was better to release the fish after catching it. "If we keep the fish we catch, there will be fewer fish each time we come here," said Amy. Amy and Chris are practicing Catch and Release. By doing this they enjoy the fun of catching fish but don't

harm the fish. They let the fish go so that other people can catch it again.

Through their concern for a small stream, Amy and Chris inspired their classmates to work for the environment and raised the consciousness of their community to care about and protect a tiny, and important, piece of the earth.

Join an environmental group soon, and get involved in their volunteer projects. You'll feel good about it. So will the earth.

❖ QUESTIONS TO ASK YOURSELF ❖

There are many environmental organizations for which to volunteer. These questions might help you decide which to choose. 1) What aspect of environmental protection interests you the most? 2) What organizations have chapters in your area? 3) Are there organizations that have volunteer programs especially for teens?

chapter
7
LEADERS OF THE ENVIRONMENTAL MOVEMENT

YOU MAY THINK THAT YOU HAVE TO BE famous before you can become a leader in working to improve the environment. Although some famous people are environmental leaders, you too can be a leader by doing something every day to improve the earth and by teaching others to follow your example.

Famous people can get more publicity for a cause because of their celebrity status. You can also get free publicity by speaking to reporters and developing relationships with them. Prepare your information carefully and attractively, and you will get the attention you deserve.

Vice-President Al Gore, is a long-time environmental leader. Before becoming Vice-President, he was a senator from Tennessee. As Senator, he tried to make other politicians aware of the earth's problems. He wrote a book entitled *Earth in the Balance*, which describes the problems the earth is facing and suggests ways to solve the problems.

One of the environmental leaders the Vice-President writes about is Chico Mendes who led the fight to stop the destruction of the rain forests. Chico Mendes was a rubber tapper in the Amazon forest of Brazil. He collected the sap from rubber trees and harvested fruits and nuts. He showed other people how to do this without harming the rain forest. Rich landowners wanted to burn down or bulldoze the remaining forests and turn them into cattle ranches.

Mendes and other rubber tappers stood in front of the bulldozers and stopped those who tried to burn the rain forest. He encouraged farmers to preserve their land and live in harmony with it. Because he blocked the attempts to destroy the rain forest, Chico Mendes was murdered by a shotgun blast as he stood in the doorway of his house. Because of Chico Mendes and his friends, the world became aware of the rain forest ecosystem and its global value.

Another leader written about in *Earth in the Balance* is Wangari Matthai, a Kenyan woman. She founded the Greenbelt Movement which organized women to plant trees in order to stop the soil erosion. People in the movement have planted over eight million trees in less than ten years. She showed the people of Kenya that trees anchored the soil and prevented it from washing or blowing away. By saving the soil, the people were able to grow more food.

The son of Chico Mendes stands near a picture of his father, who was killed because he opposed rain forest destruction.

Ordinary people worldwide are working hard to save the earth. In the United States, school groups and individual young people are actively leading the way in the fight to preserve the earth. They are setting an example for adults.

A fifth-grade class in Utah discovered a stream running through a field littered with trash, discarded building materials, and old car parts. They decided to clean the area. They studied county tax records to find the owner of the field and learned that the northern half was privately owned but the southern half was city property. The stream was the dividing line.

They consulted with experts about the plant and animal life in the field and then wrote a plan to clear the field and replant it with trees and shrubs. The class called themselves Kids Organized to Protect the Environment (KOPE). They presented their plan to the city, and it was approved by the officials.

The kids named the field Hidden Hollow and KOPE organized a one day cleanup. Over three hundred students and dozens of adult volunteers came. Despite the success of the cleanup, KOPE wanted to do more to ensure the field's protection. They persuaded the city to ban dumping and campaigned to have the field designated a nature park. KOPE reached agreements with the owners of the northern half, and the city who owned the southern half. The southern half of

In St. Louis, a group of kids call themselves the Dolphin Defenders and do cleanup projects such as collecting old tires.

the field including the stream would be protected by being re-zoned as a residential area.

This is just one example of what kids can do when they get interested in a cause.

❖ QUESTIONS TO ASK YOURSELF ❖

There are many leaders in the fight to protect the environment. You can be one too. 1) What do you think makes someone a leader? 2) Who is an environmental leader you admire? 3) What do you admire about him or her? 4) Do you have some or all of these qualities?

chapter

8

THE FUTURE

SOME SCIENTISTS AND ENVIRONMENTAL
activists have called the 1990s, the "Environmental Decade." Let us hope it is, because we
cannot afford to go backward.

There are plenty of doom and gloom predic-
tions on what will happen by the year 2000.
Scientists estimate, seventy percent of the rain
forests will be destroyed. More than one hundred plant and animal species will become
extinct each day. Half the landfills in the U.S.
will be full and twenty-five percent of the
world's drinking water will be polluted. It's up
to us to make sure this doesn't happen.

On the brighter side, concern about environmental trends appears to be growing in every
country of the world. The first Earth Summit in
1992 in Rio de Janeiro is proof that world leaders are starting to recognize the importance of a
clean environment. It is up to each of us,
though, to make sure that our political leaders
follow up their words with actions. Only by

The Earth Summit in Rio de Janeiro brought together people of many nations.

letting them know that we won't tolerate the continued abuse of the earth will they act in defense of our planet.

The membership growth in environmental groups is proof of our concern. Membership has grown from four million in 1980 to over thirteen million in 1992. It is estimated that over twenty-five million Americans are involved in local and regional environmental issues.

This concern isn't just in the United States. Another survey in 1989 covered sixteen nations. The results were similar to those in the U.S.

Soon after taking office, President Cinton and Vice-President Gore unveiled their plan to create more jobs and to protect our country's natural resources. Under it, wetlands would be maintained, more trees planted, and a jobs program created for youth in national parks and forests. Improvements would be made to mass transit, sewage treatment, and drinking water facilities. All federal buildings will upgrade their energy systems and money will be spent on research into renewable energy.

If the 1990s is to be the "Environmental Decade," it's up to us to make it happen. Each of us must take personal responsibility for our actions and be knowledgeable about how they affect the environment. We make choices every day and our choices and actions should be environmentally responsible. Individuals, community groups, corporations, and our government are

The slogan "earth day every day" is a reminder that the environment deserves our full attention.

making changes for the better through recycling, reduction of toxic air emissions, changes in land-use, education, and many other programs.

We need to involve more people. Convince your family, friends, and neighbors to take action and start working for the environment.

❖ QUESTIONS TO ASK YOURSELF ❖

Your task as a human being is to preserve the earth. Let's think about how to do that. 1) How can you educate others about the issue? 2) What changes can you make in your own household to work toward a healthy environment?

GLOSSARY

activist Someone who works very hard for a cause or idea.

aquatic Living or growing in water.

atmosphere The air around the earth.

biodiversity The overall number and variety of different species living on earth.

carbon dioxide (CO_2) The most abundant gas in the atmosphere, made up of carbon and oxygen.

ecosystem A community of living and non-living things that are interdependent.

environment The world around us and everything in it—sky, earth, water, humans, and other living things as well as everything humans have created.

fossil fuel Substances formed millions of years ago from the remains of prehistoric animals and plants—natural gas, coal, and oil.

groundwater Water that lies beneath the surface of the ground.

habitat The place where an organism lives and grows naturally.

landfill A place where garbage is put.

legislation Making or enacting laws.

methane A gas given off by decaying plants and garbage and by cattle and sheep.

nitrogen oxide A gas given off by burning fossil fuels.

organism A living thing.

oxygen A gas essential to life which is given off by plants during photosynthesis.

pesticides Chemicals used to kill pests.

photosynthesis A process by which plants use sunlight, water, and carbon dioxide to make food for themselves and release oxygen into the atmosphere.

poll A sampling or collection of opinions.

pollution Substances that dirty and poison the environment.

rainforest Dense, tropical woodlands.

recycling The reuse of materials.

scientist A person learned in a specific knowledge which relates to the physical world.

silt Fine sand or earth deposited by running water on river, lake, and stream bottoms.

species A distinct kind of animal or plant.

sulphur dioxide A gas produced by power plants, factories, and cars.

toxic Poisonous.

ultraviolet radiation A wavelength of energy from the sun.

wetlands Wet spongy land, saturated but not usually covered, with water. Wetlands used to be called swamps.

Organizations to Contact

LISTED BELOW ARE MAJOR ENVIRONMENTAL GROUPS IN the United States and Canada. The Conservation Directory, published by the National Wildlife Federation (address below), lists hundreds of national, state and local environmental groups.

American Rivers
801 Pennsylvania Ave., SE, Suite 400,
Washington, DC 20003-2167, 202-547-6900

Bass Anglers Sportsman Society
5845 Carmichael Rd., Montgomery, AL 36117,
205-272-9530

Canadian Environmental Network
P.O. Box 1289, Station B, Ottawa, ON K1P 5R3,
613-563-2078

Children of the Green Earth
Box 95219, Seattle, WA 98145

Citizens Clearinghouse For Hazardous Waste
P.O. Box 6806, Falls Church, VA 22040, 703-237-2249

Citizens for a Safe Environment
745 Queen St., East, Toronto, DN M4M 1H3,
416-462-3860

Clean Water Action
1320 18th St. NW, Washington, DC 20036, 202-457-1286

The Conservation Foundation
1250 24th St. NW, Washington, DC 20037, 202-293-4800

The Cousteau Society Inc.
930 W. 21st St., Norfolk, VA 23517, 804-627-1144

Defenders of Wildlife
1244 19th St. NW, Washington, DC 20036, 202-659-9510

Earthwatch
P.O. Box 403N, Mt. Auburn St., Watertown, MA 02272,
617-926-8200

Environmental Defense Fund, Inc.
257 Park Avenue South, New York, NY 10010,
212-505-2100

Federation of Fly Fishers
P.O. Box 1088, West Yellowstone, MT 59758,
406-646-9541

Friends of the Earth
218 D St. SE, Washington, DC 20003, 202-544-2600

Greenpeace USA, Inc.
1436 U St. NW, Washington, DC 20009, 202-462-1177

Izaak Walton League Of America
1401 Wilson Blvd., Level B, Arlington, VA 22209,
703-528-1818

National Arbor Day Foundation
100 Arbor Ave., Nebraska City, NE 68410, 402-474-5655

National Audubon Society
950 Third Avenue, New York, NY 10022, 212-546-9100

National Parks and Conservation Association
1015 31st St. NW, Washington, DC 20007-4406,
202-944-8530

The Nature Conservancy
1815 North Lynn St., Arlington, VA 22209, 703-841-5300

Natural Resources Defense Council
40 Wast 20th St., New York, NY 10011, 212-727-2700

Rainforest Action Network
301 Broadway, Suite A, San Francisco, CA 94133,
415-398-4404

Sierra Club
730 Polk St., San Francisco, CA 94109, 415-776-2211

The Wilderness Society
900 17th St. NW, Washington, DC 20006-2596
202-833-2300

World Wildlife Fund
1250 24th St. NW, Washington, DC 20037, 202-293-4800

FOR FURTHER READING

Brother Eagle, Sister Sky. New York: Dial Books, 1991.

Corson, Walter H., ed. *The Global Ecology Handbook: What You Can Do About The Environmental Crisis.* Boston: Beacon Press, 1990.

Dee, Catherine, ed. *Kid Heroes of the Environment: Simple Things Real Kids are Doing to Save The Earth.* Berkley, CA: Earth Works Press, 1991.

Earth Works Group. *50 Simple Things You Can Do To Save The Earth.* Berkley, CA: Earth Works Press, 1989.

Elkington, John, Hailes, Julia, Hill, Douglas, and Makower, Joel. *Going Green—A Kid's Handbook to Saving the Planet.* New York: Viking Penguin Publishers, 1990.

Gore, Albert. *Earth in the Balance.* Boston: Houghton-Mifflin, 1991.

Lewis, Scott. *The Rainforest Book.* Los Angeles: Living Planet Press, 1990.

Lowery, Linda. *Earth Day.* Minneapolis: Carolrhoda Books Inc., 1991.

Markle, Sandra. *The Kids' Earth Handbook.* New York: Atheneum, 1991.

Miles, Betty. *Save The Earth: An Action Handbook For Kids.* New York: Alfred A. Knopf, 1991.

Pedersen, Anne. *The Kids' Environment Book: What's Awry and Why.* Santa Fe, NM: John Muir Publications, 1991.

Steger, Will. *Saving the Earth: A Citizen's Guide to Environmental Action.* New York: Alfred A. Knopf, 1990.

INDEX

ABOUT THE AUTHOR

Robert Gartner spent twelve years with the National Park Service working on planning teams and natural resource programs for wild and scenic rivers, national trails, wilderness, grazing, fisheries, fire, and endangered species. He is a natural resource specialist for the Bureau of Indian Affairs, and lives in Burke, Virginia.

Mr. Gartner has written articles for outdoor publications, technical journals, and newspapers. He has published two books, *The National Parks Fishing Guide* and *Careers in the National Parks.*

PHOTO RESEARCH: Vera Amadzadeh
PHOTO CREDITS: © John Gayusky (p. *26*), © Randy Showstack (p. *39*), AP/Wide World Photos (all other photos)
DESIGN: Kim Sonky